Delicious
bite-size

Delicious bite-size

Love Food™ is an imprint of Parragon Books Ltd

Parragon
Queen Street House
4 Queen Street
Bath BA1 1HE, UK

Copyright © Parragon Books Ltd 2007

Love Food™ and the accompanying heart device is a trademark of Parragon Books Ltd

Introduction by Frances Eames
Photography by Günter Beer
Home Economist Stevan Paul

ISBN 978-1-4054-9559-2

Printed in China

Notes for the reader
• This book uses imperial, metric, and US cup measurements. Follow the same units of measurement throughout; do not mix imperial and metric.
• All spoon measurements are level: teaspoons are assumed to be 5 ml, and tablespoons are assumed to be 15 ml.
• Unless otherwise stated, milk is assumed to be lowfat and eggs are medium. The times given are an approximate guide only.
• Some recipes contain nuts. If you are allergic to nuts you should avoid using them and any products containing nuts.
• Recipes using raw or very lightly cooked eggs should be avoided by infants, the elderly, pregnant women, convalescents, and anyone suffering from illness.

Contents

Bite-size

A morsel of something delicious and tantalizing is all you need to make the perfect party. Bite-size entertaining is well and truly back in fashion. For gourmet menus with the minimum of effort, try the fabulous collection of recipe ideas inside this book.

Bite-size dining is great for any occasion and can be as chic or as informal as you want. Forget stuffy seating plans and polished silver flatware—this season it's all about getting fun and friendly. You could host an early evening cocktail party accompanied by a light and delicious buffet, or turn a drinks party into a real occasion with a really sumptuous spread.

Don't be daunted by making your own canapés. They are easy to prepare in advance, look fantastic, and are sure to create a good impression.

For maximum impact they should emphasize visual style as well as taste; color, shape, and texture are all important. From traditional and much-loved classics to more modern and exotic creations, this book provides a palette of flavors from across the globe.

Choosing the menu

Setting the menu is crucial to determining the mood and feel of your gathering. Think about the occasion, the season, and the guests' requirements. For a luxurious cocktail party, pick the most impressive looking dishes. If you are hosting a small and intimate gathering then you might focus the menu on your friends' favorite foods. For a summer soirée, you may decide to plan vegetable and seafood dishes for *al fresco* eating. Think about which vegetables are in season and buy them no sooner than the day

before the party to ensure that you get the freshest ingredients. Most importantly, your menu should contain a variety of colors, textures, and shapes. Don't forget to ask any vegetarian, gluten-, or dairy-intolerant diners to give you prior warning of any special requirements.

Preparation

Once you have chosen an array of delicacies you can plan your strategy. Make a list of ingredients and shop the day before. It is important to prepare what you can in advance and refrigerate. This will leave you with time to organize your home and plan what to wear. Make sure you work in an organized space; clean your counters between each dish and wash up as you go to maintain a calm and serene kitchen. You can always ask friends to prepare a specific bite and give them the recipe in advance.

Presentation

Presentation is the key to producing a breathtaking spread. Serving platters and bowls should be attractive and matching. You may want to theme the evening by using chic Japanese platters or colorful Mediterranean dishes. You could include different shaped plates and bowls, or serve food on wooden boards. All white or all black dishes can be quite striking, and they provide a simple canvas for the attractive nibbles.

If you aren't able to match the dishes then try lining them with simple but effective napkins to maintain a matching set. Keep garnishes to a minimum so as not to distract from the food. Small, practical details can make the difference between a messy eating experience and a sophisticated party. Provide small glasses for used skewers, several finger bowls with lemons, and plenty of attractive napkins.

Canapés

makes 32

2 tbsp olive oil, plus extra for brushing, and drizzling

1 onion, finely chopped

1 garlic clove, finely chopped

14 oz/400 g canned chopped tomatoes

scant 3 cups baby spinach leaves

2 tbsp pine nuts

salt and pepper

for the bread dough

4 tbsp warm water

1/2 tsp active dry yeast

pinch of sugar

generous 11/4 cups white bread flour, plus extra, for dusting

1/2 tsp salt

spanish spinach & tomato pizzas

To make the bread dough, measure the water into a small bowl, sprinkle in the dry yeast and sugar, and let stand in a warm place for 10–15 minutes, or until frothy.

Meanwhile, sift the flour and salt into a large bowl. Make a well in the center of the flour and pour in the yeast liquid, then mix together with a wooden spoon. Using your hands, work the mixture until it leaves the sides of the bowl clean.

Turn the dough out onto a lightly floured counter and knead for 10 minutes, or until smooth and elastic and no longer sticky. Shape into a ball and put it in a clean bowl. Cover with a clean, damp dish towel and let stand in a warm place for 1 hour, or until it has risen and doubled in size.

To make the topping, heat the oil in a large, heavy-bottom skillet. Add the onion and cook for 5 minutes, or until soft. Add the garlic and cook for 30 seconds. Stir in the tomatoes and cook for 5 minutes, stirring occasionally, until reduced to a thick mixture. Add the spinach leaves and cook, stirring, until wilted. Season to taste with salt and pepper.

While the dough is rising, preheat the oven to 400°F/200°C. Brush several baking sheets with olive oil. Turn the dough out onto a lightly floured counter and knead well for 2–3 minutes to knock out the air bubbles. Roll out the dough very, very thinly and, using a 2 1/2-inch/6-cm plain, round cutter, cut out 32 circles. Place on the prepared baking sheets.

Spread each base with the spinach mixture, sprinkle over the pine nuts and drizzle with a little of the olive oil. Bake in the oven for 10–15 minutes, or until the edges are golden. Serve the pizzas hot.

makes 8

1 small French baguette

4 tomatoes, thinly sliced

4 hard-cooked eggs

4 bottled or canned anchovies in olive oil, drained and halved lengthwise

8 marinated pitted black olives

for the tapenade

1/2 cup pitted black olives

6 bottled or canned anchovies in olive oil, drained

2 tbsp capers, rinsed

2 garlic cloves, coarsely chopped

1 tsp Dijon mustard

2 tbsp lemon juice

1 tsp fresh thyme leaves

4–5 tbsp olive oil

pepper

egg & tapenade toasts

To make the tapenade, place the olives, anchovies, capers, garlic, mustard, lemon juice, thyme, and pepper to taste in a food processor and process for 20–25 seconds, or until smooth. Scrape down the sides of the mixing bowl. With the motor running, gradually add the oil through the feeder tube to make a smooth paste. Spoon the paste into a bowl, cover with plastic wrap, and set aside until required.

Preheat the broiler to medium. Cut the baguette into 8 slices, discarding the crusty ends. Toast on both sides under the hot broiler until light golden brown. Let cool.

To assemble the toasts, spread a little of the tapenade on 1 side of each slice of toast. Top with the tomato slices. Shell the hard-cooked eggs, then slice and arrange over the tomatoes. Dot each egg slice with a little of the remaining tapenade and top with anchovies. Halve the marinated olives and arrange 2 halves on each toast. Serve immediately.

makes 24

4 scallions, white parts and half the green parts, very finely chopped

1/2 lemon, sliced

1 bay leaf, torn in half

1/2 tsp black peppercorns, lightly crushed

4 fl oz/125 ml dry white wine

1 lb/450 g boneless salmon, cut into pieces

4 oz/115 g butter, at room temperature

5 oz/140 g smoked salmon, cut into pieces

1/4 tsp ground nutmeg

2 tbsp very finely chopped fresh parsley

salt and pepper

12 large slices country-style bread, such as sourdough, each about 1/2 inch/1 cm thick

smoked salmon pâté

Put the scallions, lemon slices, bay leaf, peppercorns, and white wine in a large nonstick skillet, add water to half fill the pan, and bring to a boil. Boil for 2 minutes, and then reduce the heat to its lowest setting. Add the salmon pieces, cover the pan, and leave to simmer for 8 minutes. Remove the pan from the heat, keep covered, and allow the salmon to cool in the cooking liquid.

Meanwhile, melt 1 oz/30 g of the butter in a large skillet over medium heat. Add the smoked salmon pieces and nutmeg and stir for about 2 minutes, until the salmon looses its shiny coral color and becomes opaque. Remove from the heat and set aside until cool.

Drain and flake the poached salmon and put into a wide, shallow bowl. Add the smoked salmon mixture and cooking juices and the remaining butter and use your fingers to mix it all together until the salmon is very finely mixed. Stir in the parsley. Taste and adjust the seasoning, although you probably won't need much salt because of the flavor of the smoked salmon. Spoon into a bowl, cover, and chill until 30 minutes before you are ready to serve.

When you are ready to serve, preheat the broiler to high. Toast the bread on both sides until golden brown and crisp, then cut each slice in half. Spread the salmon pâté on the hot toast and serve.

serves 4

2 tbsp butter, melted,
plus extra for greasing

8 oz/225 g waxy potatoes,
finely diced

1 lb 2 oz/500 g fresh baby
spinach

2 tbsp water

1 tomato, seeded and
chopped

1/4 tsp chili powder

1/2 tsp lemon juice

8 oz/225 g (8 sheets) filo
pastry, thawed if frozen

salt and pepper

potato & spinach triangles

Preheat the oven to 375°F/190°C. Lightly grease a baking sheet with a little butter. Cook the potatoes in a pan of lightly salted boiling water for 10 minutes, or until tender. Drain thoroughly and place in a mixing bowl.

Meanwhile, put the spinach into a large skillet with the water, cover, and cook, stirring occasionally, over low heat for 2 minutes, or until wilted. Drain the spinach thoroughly, squeezing out the excess moisture, and add to the potatoes. Stir in the tomato, chili powder, and lemon juice. Season to taste with salt and pepper.

Lightly brush the sheets of filo pastry with melted butter. Spread out 4 of the sheets and lay a second sheet on top of each. Cut them into rectangles about 8 x 4 inches/20 x 10 cm.

Spoon a portion of the potato and spinach mixture onto one end of each rectangle. Fold a corner of the pastry over the filling, fold the pointed end back over the pastry strip, then fold over the remaining pastry to form a triangle.

Place the triangles on the prepared baking sheet and bake in the preheated oven for 20 minutes, or until golden brown. Serve hot or cold.

makes 20

1 thin French baguette,
cut into 20 slices

extra-virgin olive oil

*for the gorgonzola &
caramelized onion topping*

2 large onions, thinly sliced

1 oz/25 g butter

1 1/2 oz/40 g superfine sugar

8 fl oz/225 ml water

6 oz/175 g gorgonzola cheese

*for the tomato, avocado &
bacon topping*

2 oz/55 g chopped bacon

1 tbsp olive oil

1 large tomato, cored, seeded,
and finely diced

1–2 tbsp lemon juice

1–2 tbsp extra-virgin olive oil

2 tbsp finely shredded basil
leaves

pinch of sugar

1 avocado

salt and pepper

topped crostini

Preheat the broiler and place the bread slices on the broiler pan about 4 inches/10 cm from the source of the heat. Toast slowly for 6–8 minutes, turning once, until crisp and golden on both sides. Leave to cool.

To make the caramelized onions, put the onions, butter, and half the sugar in a saucepan with the water and bring to a boil. Reduce the heat and simmer, uncovered, for about 20 minutes until the onions are tender and the water has evaporated. Transfer the onions to a skillet, sprinkle with the remaining sugar, and stir over medium-high heat until the sugar melts and the onions are a light golden brown.

To make the tomato, avocado, and bacon topping, put the chopped bacon and olive oil in a skillet over medium-high heat and stir for about 5 minutes until the bacon is crisp. Remove from the skillet, drain on paper towels, and then transfer to a bowl. Add the diced tomatoes, lemon juice, olive oil, basil, sugar, and salt and pepper to taste and stir. Cut the avocado in half, remove the pit and peel, then finely dice the flesh. Add to the bowl and gently stir together, making sure the avocado is well coated so it doesn't turn brown; add extra lemon juice or olive oil, if necessary.

When ready to serve, cover 10 crostini with a small slice of gorgonzola cheese, then top with a dollop of the caramelized onions. Top the remaining crostini with the tomato, avocado, and bacon mixture. Arrange the crostini on large platters and serve.

makes 30

3 large potatoes, cut into chunks

3/4 cup frozen peas

generous 1/3 cup frozen corn kernels, thawed

2 shallots, finely chopped

1 tsp ground cumin

1 tsp ground coriander

2 fresh green chiles, seeded and finely chopped

2 tbsp chopped fresh mint

2 tbsp chopped fresh cilantro

4 tbsp lemon juice

15 sheets filo pastry (about 4 1/2 x 7 inches/ 12 x 18 cm), thawed if frozen

melted butter, for brushing

peanut or corn oil, for deep-frying

mango chutney, to serve

salt

vegetable samosas

Place the potatoes in a saucepan and add cold water to cover and a pinch of salt. Bring to a boil, then reduce the heat, cover, and let simmer for 15–20 minutes, or until tender. Meanwhile, cook the peas according to the instructions on the package, then drain. Drain the potatoes, return to the saucepan, and mash coarsely with a potato masher or fork. Add the peas to the potatoes, then transfer to a bowl.

Add the corn kernels, shallots, cumin, ground coriander, chiles, mint, fresh cilantro, and lemon juice and season to taste with salt. Mix well.

Keep the filo pastry sheets covered with plastic wrap to prevent them drying out. Take a sheet of filo, brush with melted butter, and cut in half lengthwise. Place a tablespoonful of the filling in a corner of the pastry strip. Fold the pastry over at right angles to make a triangle, enclosing the filling. Continue folding in this way all the way down the strip to make a triangular package. Repeat with the remaining filo and filling.

Heat the oil in a deep-fat fryer or large pan to 350–375°F/ 180–190°C, or until a cube of bread browns in 30 seconds. Add the samosas, in batches, and cook until golden brown. Remove with a slotted spoon and drain on paper towels. Alternatively, bake the samosas in a preheated oven at 400°F/200°C for 10–15 minutes, or until golden brown. Serve the samosas hot or at room temperature with mango chutney.

makes 72

4 skinless, boneless chicken thighs

3¹/2 oz/100 g cooked, shelled shrimp

1 small egg, beaten

3 scallions, finely chopped

2 garlic cloves, crushed

2 tbsp chopped fresh cilantro

1 tbsp fish sauce

12 slices white bread, crusts removed

generous ¹/3 cup sesame seeds

corn oil, for pan-frying

salt and pepper

shredded scallion curls, to garnish

shrimp & chicken sesame toasts

Place the chicken and shrimp in a food processor and process until very finely chopped. Add the egg, scallions, garlic, cilantro, fish sauce, and salt and pepper to taste, and pulse for a few seconds to mix well. Transfer to a large bowl.

Spread the mixture evenly over the slices of bread, right to the edges. Sprinkle the sesame seeds over a plate and press the chicken-and-shrimp-topped side of each slice of bread into them to coat evenly.

Using a sharp knife, cut the bread into small squares, making 6 per slice.

Heat a ¹/2-inch/1-cm depth of oil in a wide skillet until very hot. Pan-fry the bread rectangles quickly, in batches, for 2–3 minutes, or until golden brown all over, turning them once.

Drain the toasts well on paper towels, transfer to a serving dish, and garnish with shredded scallion curls. Serve hot.

makes 12

4 oz/115 g ready-prepared
puff pastry rolled to a depth
of 1/8 inch/3 mm

4 large fresh scallops,
cleaned and roes removed

salt and pepper

extra-virgin olive oil,
for coating

for the pea and mint purée

2 oz/55 g cooked peas

small garlic clove, grated

1 tbsp extra-virgin olive oil

1 tbsp chopped mint

1 tbsp sour cream

1 tsp lemon juice

salt and pepper

mini tartlets with scallops & pea & mint purée

Preheat the oven to 350°F/180°C. Using a 1½-inch/4-cm round cookie cutter, cut out 12 pastry rounds. Re-roll and use the leftovers if there is not enough pastry to make 12 rounds.

Place the rounds on a cookie sheet lined with wax paper. Place another layer of wax paper on top, and then place a slightly smaller cookie sheet on top of this. (This will prevent the pastry from rising in the oven.)

Set aside the pastry rounds to rest in a cool place for 20 minutes, then cook in the oven for 15–20 minutes, or until golden. Remove from the oven and let cool.

To make the pea and mint purée, blend the peas in a food processor and add the garlic, olive oil, mint, sour cream, lemon juice, and salt and pepper to taste. Process until combined. Scrape the mixture into a small container and place in the refrigerator.

Heat a non-stick skillet until just smoking. Toss the scallops in a little olive oil and season with salt and pepper. Add the scallops to the skillet and cook for 30 seconds each side. Remove the scallops from the pan and set aside.

To assemble the canapés, place a small amount of pea and mint purée on each tartlet. Cut each scallop into 3 slices and arrange on top of the canapés. Serve.

Elegant Nibbles

serves 6–8

4 large skinless, boneless chicken breasts

5 tbsp olive oil

1 onion, finely chopped

6 garlic cloves, finely chopped

grated rind of 1 lemon, finely pared rind of 1 lemon and juice of both lemons

4 tbsp chopped fresh flat-leaf parsley

salt and pepper

lemon wedges and crusty bread, to serve

chicken in lemon & garlic

Using a sharp knife, slice the chicken breasts widthwise into very thin slices. Heat the olive oil in a large, heavy-bottom skillet, add the onion and cook for 5 minutes, or until softened but not browned. Add the garlic and cook for an additional 30 seconds.

Add the sliced chicken to the skillet and cook gently for 5–10 minutes, stirring from time to time, until all the ingredients are lightly browned and the chicken is tender.

Add the grated lemon rind and the lemon juice and let it bubble. At the same time, deglaze the skillet by scraping and stirring all the bits on the bottom of the skillet into the juices with a wooden spoon. Remove the skillet from the heat, stir in the parsley, and season to taste with salt and pepper.

Transfer the chicken in lemon and garlic, piping hot, to a warmed serving dish. Sprinkle with the pared lemon rind, and serve with lemon wedges for squeezing over the chicken, accompanied by chunks or slices of crusty bread for mopping up the lemon and garlic juices.

makes 12

12 oz/350 g monkfish tail or
9 oz/250 g monkfish fillet

12 stalks of fresh rosemary

3 tbsp olive oil

juice of 1/2 small lemon

1 garlic clove, crushed

salt and pepper

6 thick slices Canadian bacon

aïoli (see page 87), to serve

monkfish, rosemary & bacon skewers

If using monkfish tail, cut either side of the central bone with a sharp knife and remove the flesh to form 2 fillets. Slice the fillets in half lengthwise, then cut each fillet into 12 bite-size chunks to give a total of 24 pieces. Put the monkfish pieces in a large bowl.

To prepare the rosemary skewers, strip the leaves off the stalks and set them aside, leaving a few leaves at one end.

For the marinade, finely chop the reserved leaves and whisk together in a bowl with the olive oil, lemon juice, garlic, and salt and pepper to taste. Add the monkfish pieces and toss until coated in the marinade. Cover and let marinate in the refrigerator for 1–2 hours.

Preheat the broiler to medium-high and arrange the skewers on the broiler pan so that the leaves of the rosemary skewers protrude from the broiler and therefore do not catch fire during cooking. Broil the monkfish and bacon skewers for 10 minutes, turning from time to time and basting with any remaining marinade, or until cooked. Serve hot accompanied by a bowl of aïoli in which to dip them.

smoked salmon blinis

makes 24

for the blinis

3 oz/85 g all-purpose flour

1 tsp active dry yeast

1/2 tsp sugar

5 fl oz/150 ml warm water

3 oz/85 g buckwheat flour

4 fl oz/125 ml warm milk

1 1/2 oz/40 g butter, melted and cooled

1 large egg, separated

vegetable oil, for cooking

salt and pepper

for the topping

3 oz/85 g sour cream

finely grated rind of 2 lemons

2 oz/55 g smoked salmon, very finely sliced

pepper

2 tbsp very finely snipped chives, to garnish

To make the blinis, stir the all-purpose flour, yeast, and sugar together in a bowl. Make a well in the center and slowly add the water, drawing in flour from the side to make a wet, lumpy batter. Beat until the batter is smooth, then stir in the buckwheat flour, cover the bowl tightly with a kitchen towel, and set aside for 1 hour, until the batter has risen and the surface is covered with air bubbles.

Meanwhile, mix the sour cream with the lemon rind and pepper to taste. Cover and chill until ready to use. Stir the milk, butter, and egg yolk together with a generous pinch of salt and pepper, then add to the batter, stirring well until blended. Beat the egg white in a separate bowl until soft peaks form, and then fold into the batter.

Heat a large nonstick skillet over medium heat until you can feel the heat rising, then lightly brush the surface all over with vegetable oil using a crumpled paper towel. Fill a tablespoon measure two-thirds full with the batter, then drop the batter onto the hot surface so it forms a circle about 2 inches/5 cm across; add as many more as will fit in the pan without touching. Cook for just over a minute, or until the top surface is covered with air holes and the bottom is golden brown and set. Use a palette knife to flip over the blinis and cook until set and golden brown. Transfer to a heatproof plate and keep warm in a low oven while you cook the remaining batter.

To serve, arrange the warm, not hot, blinis on a platter and top each with about 2 teaspoons of the chilled sour cream. Lay the salmon strips over the sour cream, add a little piece of chive to each, and serve.

makes 24

3 medium-sized heads
chicory

4 oz/125 g bleu cheese, such
as Stilton, finely crumbled

4 tbsp pecan halves,
very finely chopped

snipped cress, to garnish

for the dressing

3¹/2 fl oz/100 ml extra-virgin
olive oil

2¹/2 tbsp balsamic vinegar

1 tsp Dijon mustard

1 tsp sugar

salt and pepper

pretty chicory bites

To make the dressing, put the oil, vinegar, mustard, sugar, and
salt and pepper to taste in a screw-top jar and shake until
blended. Taste and adjust the seasoning, then set aside until
ready to use.

Cut the edges off the chicory heads so you can separate the
leaves. Pick over the leaves and select the 24 best, boat-shaped
leaves, then rinse them and pat dry.

Put the cheese and pecans in a bowl and gently toss together.
Add 2 tablespoons of the dressing and toss again.

Arrange the chicory leaves on serving platters, then put a
teaspoon of the cheese and pecans toward the pointed end
of each leaf. Add some snipped cress to each chicory leaf to
garnish. Cover and chill for up to an hour before serving.

serves 6

1 lb/450 g prepared squid

all-purpose flour, for coating

corn oil, for deep-frying

salt

lemon wedges, to garnish

aïoli (see page 87), to serve

calamares

Slice the squid into ½-inch/1-cm rings and halve the tentacles if large. Rinse and dry well on paper towels so that they do not spit during cooking. Dust the squid rings with flour so that they are lightly coated. Do not season the flour as seasoning squid with salt before cooking toughens it.

Heat the corn oil in a deep-fryer to 350–375°F/180–190°C, or until a cube of bread browns in 30 seconds. Carefully add the squid rings, in batches so that the temperature of the oil does not drop, and deep-fry for 2–3 minutes, or until golden brown and crisp all over, turning several times. Do not overcook as the squid will become tough and rubbery rather than moist and tender.

Using a slotted spoon, remove the deep-fried squid from the deep-fryer and drain well on paper towels. Transfer to a warm oven while you deep-fry the remaining squid rings.

Sprinkle the deep-fried squid with salt and serve piping hot, garnished with lemon wedges for squeezing over them. Accompany with a bowl of aïoli in which to dip the pieces.

serves 6–8

7 oz/200 g Manchego cheese

3 tbsp all-purpose flour

1 egg

1 tsp water

1¹⁄₂ cups fresh white or
brown bread crumbs

corn oil, for deep-frying

salt and pepper

deep-fried manchego cheese

Slice the cheese into triangular shapes about ¾ inch/2 cm thick or alternatively into cubes measuring about the same size. Put the flour in a plastic bag and season with salt and pepper to taste. Break the egg into a shallow dish and beat together with the water. Spread the bread crumbs onto a plate.

Toss the cheese pieces in the flour so that they are evenly coated, then dip the cheese in the egg mixture. Finally, dip the cheese in the bread crumbs so that the pieces are coated on all sides. Transfer to a large plate and store in the refrigerator until you are ready to serve them.

Just before serving, heat about 1 inch/2.5 cm of the corn oil in a large, heavy-bottom skillet or heat the oil in a deep-fryer to 350–375°F/180–190°C, or until a cube of bread browns in 30 seconds. Add the cheese pieces, in batches of about 4 or 5 pieces so that the temperature of the oil does not drop, and deep-fry for 1–2 minutes, turning once, until the cheese is just starting to melt and they are golden brown on all sides. Do make sure that the oil is hot enough, otherwise the coating on the cheese will take too long to become crisp and the cheese inside may ooze out.

Using a slotted spoon, remove the deep-fried cheese from the skillet or deep-fryer and drain well on paper towels. Serve the deep-fried cheese pieces hot, accompanied by toothpicks on which to spear them.

serves 8

1 lb 12 oz/800 g fresh
mussels, in their shells

splash of dry white wine

1 bay leaf

3 oz/85 g butter

generous 1/2 cup fresh white
or brown bread crumbs

4 tbsp chopped fresh

flat-leaf parsley, plus extra
sprigs to garnish

2 tbsp snipped fresh chives

2 garlic cloves, finely chopped

salt and pepper

lemon wedges, to serve

mussels with herb & garlic butter

Clean the mussels by scrubbing or scraping the shells and pulling out any beards that are attached to them. Discard any with broken shells and any that refuse to close when tapped. Put the mussels in a strainer and rinse well under cold running water. Preheat the oven to 450°F/230°C.

Put the mussels in a large pan and add a splash of wine and the bay leaf. Cook, covered, over high heat for 5 minutes, shaking the pan occasionally, or until the mussels are opened. Drain the mussels and discard any that remain closed.

Shell the mussels, reserving one half of each shell. Arrange the mussels, in their half shells, in a large, shallow, ovenproof serving dish.

Melt the butter and pour into a small bowl. Add the bread crumbs, parsley, chives, garlic, and salt and pepper to taste and mix well together. Let stand until the butter has set slightly. Using your fingers or 2 teaspoons, take a large pinch of the herb and butter mixture and use to fill each mussel shell, pressing it down well. You can chill the filled mussels in the refrigerator at this point until ready to serve.

To serve, bake the mussels in the oven for 10 minutes, or until hot. Serve immediately, garnished with parsley sprigs, and accompanied by lemon wedges for squeezing over them.

makes 12

1 lb/450 g lean boneless pork

3 tbsp olive oil, plus extra for oiling (optional)

grated rind and juice of 1 large lemon

2 garlic cloves, crushed

2 tbsp chopped fresh flat-leaf parsley, plus extra to garnish

1 tbsp ras-el-hanout spice blend

salt and pepper

miniature pork brochettes

The brochettes are marinated overnight, so remember to do this in advance in order that they are ready when you need them. Cut the pork into pieces about ¾ inch/2 cm square and put in a large, shallow, nonmetallic dish that will hold the pieces in a single layer.

To prepare the marinade, put all the remaining ingredients in a bowl and mix well together. Pour the marinade over the pork and toss the meat in it until well coated. Cover the dish and let marinate in the refrigerator for 8 hours or overnight, stirring the pork 2–3 times.

You can use wooden or metal skewers to cook the brochettes and for this recipe you will need 12 x 6-inch/15-cm skewers. If you are using wooden ones, soak them in cold water for about 30 minutes prior to using. This helps to stop them burning and the food sticking to them during cooking. Metal skewers simply need to be greased, and flat ones should be used in preference to round ones to prevent the food on them falling off.

Preheat the broiler to medium-high. Thread 3 marinated pork pieces, leaving a little space between each piece, onto each prepared skewer. Cook the brochettes for 10–15 minutes, or until tender and lightly charred, turning several times and basting with the remaining marinade during cooking. Serve the pork brochettes piping hot, garnished with parsley.

makes 12

3 slices Parma ham

3 eggs

1 poached chicken breast,
shredded

12 Boston lettuce leaves

6 anchovies, cut in half
lengthwise

12 Parmesan shavings

cracked black pepper

for the dressing

1 tbsp mayonnaise

1 tbsp water

1 tsp white wine vinegar

miniature caesar salad

Preheat the broiler to medium–high and line the broiler rack with foil.

Place the Parma ham on the broiler rack, directly beneath the heat source, and cook until crisp. This will not take long.

Meanwhile, bring a small saucepan of water to a boil, add the eggs, and cook for 9 minutes. Cool the eggs under cold running water, then peel and roughly chop them.

To make the dressing, mix together the mayonnaise, water, and vinegar.

To assemble, place a small amount of the chicken on each lettuce leaf and top with the dressing.

Add the egg, anchovies, and Parmesan cheese and sprinkle with pepper.

Tear the Parma ham into 12 neat pieces, place a piece on top of each canapé, and serve.

serves 6

2 fresh tuna steaks, weighing
about 9 oz/250 g in total and
about 1 inch/2.5 cm thick

5 tbsp olive oil

3 tbsp red wine vinegar

4 sprigs of fresh thyme, plus
extra to garnish

1 bay leaf

2 tbsp all-purpose flour

1 onion, finely chopped

2 garlic cloves, finely chopped

1/2 cup pimiento-stuffed
green olives, halved

salt and pepper

tuna with pimiento-stuffed olives

Don't get caught out with this recipe—the tuna steaks need to be marinated, so remember to start preparing the dish the day before you are going to serve it. Remove the skin from the tuna steaks, then cut the steaks in half along the grain of the fish. Cut each half into 1/2-inch/1-cm thick slices against the grain.

Put 3 tablespoons of the olive oil and the vinegar in a large, shallow, nonmetallic dish. Strip the leaves from the sprigs of thyme and add these to the dish with the bay leaf and salt and pepper to taste. Add the prepared strips of tuna, cover the dish, and let marinate in the refrigerator for 8 hours or overnight.

The next day, put the flour in a plastic bag. Remove the tuna strips from the marinade, reserving the marinade for later, add them to the bag of flour and toss well until they are lightly coated.

Heat the remaining olive oil in a large, heavy-bottom skillet. Add the onion and garlic and gently cook for 5–10 minutes, or until softened and golden brown. Add the tuna strips to the skillet and cook for 2–5 minutes, turning several times, until the fish becomes opaque. Add the reserved marinade and olives to the skillet and cook for an additional 1–2 minutes, stirring, until the fish is tender and the sauce has thickened.

Serve the tuna and olives piping hot, garnished with thyme sprigs.

Classic Bites

serves 4

1/2 cup extra-virgin olive oil

1 small oval-shaped loaf
of white bread (ciabatta or
bloomer), cut into 1/2-inch/
1-cm slices

4 tomatoes, seeded and diced

6 fresh basil leaves, torn, plus
extra for garnish

8 black olives, pitted and
chopped

1 large garlic clove, peeled
and halved

salt and pepper

olive & tomato bruschetta

Pour half the oil into a shallow dish and place the bread in it.
Let stand for 1–2 minutes, then turn and leave for an additional
2 minutes. The bread should be thoroughly saturated in oil.

Meanwhile, put the tomatoes into a mixing bowl. Sprinkle the
basil leaves over the tomatoes. Season to taste with salt and
pepper and add the olives. Pour over the remaining oil and let
marinate while you toast the bruschetta.

Preheat the broiler to medium. Place the bread on the broiler rack
and cook for 2 minutes on each side, or until golden and crisp.

Remove the bread from the broiler and arrange on a plate.

Rub the cut edge of the garlic halves over the surface of the
bruschetta, then top each slice with a spoonful of the tomato
mixture. Serve at once, garnished with basil leaves.

makes 16

1 potato, cut into chunks

4 scallions, chopped

1 garlic clove, chopped

1 tbsp chopped fresh thyme

1 tbsp chopped fresh basil

1 tbsp chopped fresh cilantro

8 oz/225 g white crabmeat, drained if canned and thawed if frozen

1/2 tsp Dijon mustard

1/2 fresh green chile, seeded and finely chopped

1 egg, lightly beaten

all-purpose flour, for dusting

corn oil, for frying

salt and pepper

lime wedges, to garnish

dip or salsa of choice, to serve

crab cakes

Place the potato in a small pan and add water to cover. Add a pinch of salt. Bring to a boil, then reduce the heat, cover, and let simmer for 10–15 minutes, or until softened. Drain well, turn into a large bowl and mash with a potato masher or fork until smooth.

Meanwhile, place the scallions, garlic, thyme, basil, and cilantro in a mortar and pound with a pestle until smooth. Add the herb paste to the mashed potato with the crabmeat, mustard, chile, egg, and pepper to taste. Mix well, cover with plastic wrap, and let chill in the refrigerator for 30 minutes.

Sprinkle flour onto a shallow plate. Shape spoonfuls of the crabmeat mixture into small balls with your hands, then flatten slightly and dust with flour, shaking off any excess. Heat the oil in a skillet over high heat, add the crab cakes, in batches, and cook for 2–3 minutes on each side until golden. Remove from the skillet and drain on paper towels. Set aside to cool to room temperature.

Arrange the crab cakes on a serving dish and garnish with lime wedges. Serve with a bowl of dip or salsa.

meatballs in almond sauce

2 oz/55 g white or brown bread, crusts removed

3 tbsp water

2 cups fresh lean ground pork

1 large onion, finely chopped

1 garlic clove, crushed

2 tbsp chopped fresh flat-leaf parsley, plus extra to garnish

1 egg, beaten

freshly grated nutmeg

flour, for coating

2 tbsp olive oil

squeeze of lemon juice

salt and pepper

crusty bread, to serve

for the almond sauce

2 tbsp olive oil

1 oz/25 g white or brown bread

2/3 cup blanched almonds

2 garlic cloves, finely chopped

2/3 cup dry white wine

scant 2 cups vegetable stock

salt and pepper

To make the meatballs, put the bread in a bowl, add water and soak for 5 minutes. With your hands, squeeze out the water and return the bread to a dry bowl. Add the pork, onion, garlic, parsley and egg, then season with nutmeg, and salt and pepper. Knead the ingredients together to form a smooth mixture.

Spread some flour on a plate. With floured hands, shape the meat mixture into about 30 equal-size balls, then roll each meatball in flour until coated.

Heat the olive oil in a large, heavy-bottom skillet, add the meatballs, in batches so that they do not overcrowd the skillet, and cook for 4–5 minutes, or until browned on all sides. Using a slotted spoon, remove the meatballs from the skillet and set aside.

To make the almond sauce, heat the oil in the same skillet in which the meatballs were cooked. Break the bread into pieces, add to the skillet with the almonds and cook, stirring frequently, until the bread and almonds are golden. Add the garlic and cook for 30 seconds, then pour in the wine and boil for 1–2 minutes. Season to taste with salt and pepper and let cool.

Transfer the almond mixture to a food processor. Pour in the vegetable stock and blend the mixture until smooth. Return the sauce to the skillet.

Carefully add the cooked meatballs to the sauce and simmer for 25 minutes, or until the meatballs are tender. Taste and season with salt and pepper if necessary. Transfer the cooked meatballs and sauce to a warmed serving dish, add a squeeze of lemon and garnish with chopped parsley. Serve hot accompanied by slices of crusty bread.

serves 12

scant 1³/₄ cups long-grain rice

1 lb/450 g vine leaves, rinsed
if preserved in brine

2 onions, finely chopped

1 bunch scallions, finely
chopped

1 bunch fresh parsley, finely
chopped

2 tbsp fresh mint, finely
chopped

1 tbsp fennel seeds

1 tsp crushed dried chiles

finely grated rind of 2 lemons

1 cup olive oil

2¹/₂ cups boiling water

salt

stuffed vine leaves

Bring a large pan of lightly salted water to a boil. Add the rice and
return to a boil. Reduce the heat and let simmer for 15 minutes,
or until tender.

Meanwhile, if using preserved vine leaves, place them in a
heatproof bowl and pour over boiling water to cover. Set aside
to soak for 10 minutes. If using fresh vine leaves, bring a pan of
water to a boil, add the vine leaves, then reduce the heat and let
simmer for 10 minutes.

Drain the rice and, while still hot, mix with the onions, scallions,
parsley, mint, fennel seeds, chiles, lemon rind, and 3 tablespoons
of the oil in a large bowl. Season to taste with salt.

Drain the vine leaves well. Spread out 1 leaf, vein-side up, on a
counter. Place a generous teaspoonful of the rice mixture on the
leaf near the stalk. Fold the stalk end over the filling, fold in the
sides and roll up the leaf. Repeat until all the filling has been
used. There may be some vine leaves left over—you can use
them to line a serving platter, if wished.

Place the packages in a large, heavy-bottom pan in a single layer
(you may need to use 2 pans). Spoon over the remaining oil,
then add the boiling water. Cover the packages with an inverted
heatproof plate to keep them below the surface of the water,
cover the pan, and let simmer for 1 hour.

Allow the packages to cool to room temperature in the pan, then
transfer to a serving platter with a slotted spoon.

makes 40

2 oz/55 g canned anchovies
in olive oil, drained and
coarsely chopped

1/3 cup black olives, pitted
and coarsely chopped

4 oz/115 g Manchego or
Cheddar cheese, finely grated

3/4 cup all-purpose flour, plus
extra for dusting

4 oz/115 g unsalted butter,
diced

1/2 tsp cayenne pepper, plus
extra for dusting

anchovy, olive & cheese triangles

Place the anchovies, olives, cheese, flour, butter, and cayenne pepper in a food processor and pulse until a dough forms. Turn out and shape into a ball. Wrap in foil and let chill in the refrigerator for 30 minutes.

Preheat the oven to 400°F/200°C. Unwrap the dough, knead on a lightly floured counter, and roll out thinly. Using a sharp knife, cut it into strips about 2 inches/5 cm wide. Cut diagonally across each strip, turning the knife in alternate directions, to make triangles.

Arrange the triangles on 2 baking sheets and dust lightly with cayenne pepper. Bake in the preheated oven for 10 minutes, or until golden brown. Transfer to wire racks to cool completely.

makes 16

8 large eggs

2 whole pimientos (sweet red peppers) from a jar or can

8 green olives

5 tbsp mayonnaise

8 drops Tabasco sauce

large pinch cayenne pepper

salt and pepper

paprika, for dusting

sprigs of fresh dill, to garnish

deviled eggs

To cook the eggs, put them in a pan, cover with cold water, and slowly bring to a boil. Immediately reduce the heat to very low, cover, and let simmer gently for 10 minutes. As soon as the eggs are cooked, drain, and put under cold running water. By doing this quickly, you will prevent a black ring from forming round the egg yolk. Gently tap the eggs to crack the eggshells and let them stand until cold. When cold, crack the shells all over and remove them.

Using a stainless steel knife, halve the eggs lengthwise, then carefully remove the yolks. Put the yolks in a nylon strainer, set over a bowl, and rub through, then mash them with a wooden spoon or fork. If necessary, rinse the egg whites under cold water and dry very carefully.

Put the pimientos on paper towels to dry well, then chop them finely, reserving a few strips. Finely chop the olives. If you are going to pipe the filling into the eggs, you need to chop both these ingredients very finely so that they will go through a $1/2$-inch/ 1-cm tip. Add the chopped pimientos and most of the chopped olives to the mashed egg yolks, reserving 16 larger pieces for garnish. Add the mayonnaise, mix well together, then add the Tabasco sauce, cayenne pepper, and salt and pepper to taste.

Using a teaspoon, spoon the prepared filling into each egg half. Arrange the eggs on a serving plate and add a small strip of the reserved pimientos and a piece of olive to the top of each stuffed egg. Garnish with dill sprigs and serve.

serves 8

1 lb/450 g can or jar unpitted
large green olives, drained

4 garlic cloves, peeled

2 tsp coriander seeds

1 small lemon

4 sprigs of fresh thyme

4 feathery stalks of fennel

2 small fresh red chiles
(optional)

extra-virgin olive oil, to cover

pepper

cracked marinated olives

To allow the flavors of the marinade to penetrate the olives, place on a cutting board and, using a rolling pin, bash them lightly so that they crack slightly. Alternatively, use a sharp knife to cut a lengthwise slit in each olive as far as the pit. Using the flat side of a broad knife, lightly crush each garlic clove. Using a mortar and pestle, crack the coriander seeds. Cut the lemon, with its rind, into small chunks.

Put the olives, garlic, coriander seeds, lemon chunks, thyme sprigs, fennel, and chiles, if using, in a large bowl and toss together. Season with pepper to taste, but you should not need to add salt as preserved olives are usually salty enough. Pack the ingredients tightly into a glass jar with a lid. Pour in enough olive oil to cover the olives, then seal the jar tightly.

Let the olives stand at room temperature for 24 hours, then marinate in the refrigerator for at least 1 week but preferably 2 weeks before serving. From time to time, gently give the jar a shake to remix the ingredients. Return the olives to room temperature and remove from the oil to serve. Provide toothpicks for spearing the olives.

serves 6

1 lb/450 g white mushrooms

5 tbsp olive oil

2 garlic cloves, finely chopped

squeeze of lemon juice

4 tbsp chopped fresh flat-leaf parsley

salt and pepper

crusty bread, to serve

sautéed garlic mushrooms

Wipe or brush clean the mushrooms, then trim off the stalks close to the caps. Cut any large mushrooms in half or into quarters. Heat the olive oil in a large, heavy-bottom skillet, add the garlic and cook for 30 seconds–1 minute, or until lightly browned. Add the mushrooms and sauté over high heat, stirring most of the time, until the mushrooms have absorbed all the oil in the skillet.

Reduce the heat to low. When the juices have come out of the mushrooms, increase the heat again, and sauté for 4–5 minutes, stirring most of the time, until the juices have almost evaporated. Add a squeeze of lemon juice and season to taste with salt and pepper. Stir in the parsley and cook for an additional minute.

Transfer the sautéed mushrooms to a warmed serving dish and serve piping hot or warm. Accompany with chunks or slices of crusty bread for mopping up the garlic cooking juices.

serves 6–8

1 lb/450 g baby new potatoes

1 tbsp chopped fresh flat-leaf parsley

salt

for the aïoli

see page 87 for ingredients and method

baby potatoes with aïoli

To make the aïoli, follow the method on page 87. However, for this recipe the aïoli should be a little thinner so that it coats the potatoes. To ensure this, quickly blend in 1 tablespoon of water so that it forms the consistency of sauce.

To prepare the potatoes, cut them in half or quarters to make bite-size pieces. If they are very small, you can leave them whole. Put the potatoes in a large pan of cold, salted water and bring to a boil. Lower the heat and let simmer for 7 minutes, or until just tender. Drain well, then turn out into a large bowl.

While the potatoes are still warm, pour over the aïoli sauce, and gently toss the potatoes in it. Adding the sauce to the potatoes while they are still warm will help them to absorb the garlic flavor. Let stand for about 20 minutes to allow the potatoes to marinate in the sauce.

Transfer the potatoes with aïoli to a warmed serving dish, sprinkle over the parsley and salt to taste, and serve warm. Alternatively, the aïoli can be served separately, allowing diners to dip the potatoes themselves.

serves 6

4 limes

12 raw jumbo shrimp,
in their shells

3 tbsp olive oil

2 garlic cloves, finely chopped

splash of fino sherry

4 tbsp chopped fresh flat-leaf
parsley

salt and pepper

lime-drizzled shrimp

Grate the rind and squeeze the juice from 2 of the limes. Cut the remaining 2 limes into wedges and set aside for later.

To prepare the shrimp, remove the head and legs, leaving the shells and tails intact. Using a sharp knife, make a shallow slit along the underside of each shrimp, then pull out the dark vein and discard. Rinse the shrimp under cold water and dry well on paper towels.

Heat the olive oil in a large, heavy-bottom skillet, then add the garlic and cook for 30 seconds. Add the shrimp and cook for 5 minutes, stirring from time to time, or until they turn pink and start to curl. Mix in the lime rind, juice, and a splash of sherry to moisten, then stir well together.

Transfer the cooked shrimp to a serving dish, season to taste with salt and pepper, and sprinkle with the parsley. Serve piping hot, accompanied by the reserved lime wedges for squeezing over the shrimp.

Dips & Spreads

serves 6

1²/₃ cups cooked or drained canned garbanzo beans

²/₃ cup tahini, well stirred

²/₃ cup olive oil, plus extra to serve

2 garlic cloves, coarsely chopped

6 tbsp lemon juice

1 tbsp chopped fresh mint

salt and pepper

1 tsp paprika

hummus

Put the garbanzo beans, tahini, olive oil, and ²/₃ cup water into the blender and process briefly. Add the garlic, lemon juice, and mint and process until smooth.

Check the consistency of the hummus and, if it is too thick, add 1 tablespoon water and process again. Continue adding water, 1 tablespoon at a time, until the right consistency is achieved. Hummus should have a thick, coating consistency. Season with salt and pepper.

Spoon the hummus into a serving dish. Make a shallow hollow in the top and drizzle with 2–3 tablespoons olive oil. Cover with plastic wrap and chill until required. To serve, dust lightly with paprika.

serves 6

2 slices white bread, crusts removed

5 tbsp milk

8 oz smoked cod's roe

2 garlic cloves, coarsely chopped

2/3 cup olive oil

2 tbsp lemon juice

2 tbsp strained plain yogurt

pepper

black olives, to garnish

taramasalata

Tear the bread into pieces and place in a shallow bowl. Add the milk and set aside to soak. Meanwhile, using a sharp knife, scrape the cod's roe away from the outer skin.

Tip the bread and milk into the blender and process until smooth. Add the cod's roe and garlic and process again. With the motor running, gradually pour in the olive oil through the hole in the lid. Process until smooth and the consistency of mayonnaise.

Add the lemon juice and yogurt and season with pepper. Process very briefly to mix, then scrape into a bowl. Cover with plastic wrap and chill in the refrigerator until required. Garnish with black olives just before serving.

serves 6

juice of 1 lime

3 avocados

2 garlic cloves, chopped

3 scallions, chopped

2 fresh green chiles, seeded
and chopped

2 tbsp olive oil

1 tbsp sour cream

salt

cayenne pepper, to garnish

tortilla chips, to serve

guacamole

Put the lime juice into the blender. Halve the avocados and remove the pits. Scoop out the avocado flesh with a spoon straight into the blender.

Add the garlic, scallions, chiles, olive oil, and sour cream and season with salt. Process until smooth. Taste and adjust the seasoning with more salt or lime juice.

Spoon the guacamole into a serving dish. Dust lightly with cayenne pepper and serve with tortilla chips.

serves 6–8

2 large eggplants

2 red bell peppers

4 tbsp olive oil

2 garlic cloves, coarsely chopped

grated rind and juice of 1/2 lemon

1 tbsp chopped fresh cilantro

1/2–1 tsp paprika

salt and pepper

bread or toast, to serve

eggplant & bell pepper dip

Preheat the oven to 375°F/190°C. Prick the skins of the eggplants and bell peppers all over with a fork and brush with about 1 tablespoon of the olive oil. Put on a baking sheet and bake in the oven for 45 minutes, or until the skins are starting to turn black, the flesh of the eggplant is very soft, and the bell peppers are deflated.

When the vegetables are cooked, put them in a bowl and immediately cover tightly with a clean, damp dish towel. Alternatively, you can put the vegetables in a plastic bag. Let them stand for about 15 minutes, until they are cool enough to handle.

When the vegetables have cooled, cut the eggplants in half lengthwise, carefully scoop out the flesh, and discard the skin. Cut the eggplant flesh into large chunks. Remove and discard the stem, core, and seeds from the bell peppers and cut the flesh into large pieces.

Heat the remaining olive oil in a large, heavy-bottom skillet, add the eggplant flesh and bell pepper pieces and cook for 5 minutes. Add the garlic and cook for an additional 30 seconds.

Turn all the contents of the skillet onto paper towels to drain, then transfer to the bowl of a food processor. Add the lemon rind and juice, the chopped cilantro, the paprika, and salt and pepper according to taste, and blend until a speckled purée is formed.

Turn the eggplant and bell pepper dip into a serving bowl. Serve warm, at room temperature, or let cool for 30 minutes, then let chill in the refrigerator for at least 1 hour and serve cold. Accompany with thick slices of bread or toast for dipping.

serves 6

8 oz chicken livers

2/3 cup butter

2 garlic cloves, coarsely chopped

2 tsp chopped fresh sage leaves

2 tbsp Marsala wine

2/3 cup heavy cream

salt and pepper

1/4 cup butter and 4–6 fresh sage leaves, to garnish

chicken liver pâté

Trim the chicken livers and chop coarsely. Melt ½ cup of the butter in a heavy skillet. Add the chicken livers and cook over medium heat for 5–8 minutes until browned all over but still pink inside. Remove the skillet from the heat.

Transfer the chicken livers, in small batches, to the blender and process. Return all the livers to the blender and add the garlic, sage leaves, and remaining butter. Season with salt and pepper.

Pour the Marsala into the skillet and stir with a wooden spoon, scraping up any sediment, then add the mixture to the blender. Process until the pâté is smooth and thoroughly mixed. Add the cream and process again to mix. Spoon the pâté into individual pots and let cool completely.

Melt the butter for the garnish in a small pan over low heat. Remove the pan from the heat and pour the melted butter over the surface of the cooled pâté. Arrange the sage leaves on top. Let cool, then cover with plastic wrap, and chill for at least 1 hour.

makes about ¾ cup

3½ oz canned anchovy fillets

12 oz black olives, pitted and
coarsely chopped

2 garlic cloves, coarsely
chopped

2 tbsp capers, drained and
rinsed

1 tbsp Dijon mustard

3 tbsp extra-virgin olive oil

2 tbsp lemon juice

tapenade

Drain the anchovies, reserving the oil from the can. Coarsely
chop the fish and place in the blender. Add the reserved oil and
all the remaining ingredients. Process to a smooth purée. Stop
and scrape down the sides if necessary.

Transfer the tapenade to a dish, cover with plastic wrap, and
chill in the refrigerator until required. If you are not planning to
use the tapenade until the following day (or even the one after),
cover the surface with a layer of olive oil to prevent it from
drying out.

serves 6

2 red bell peppers, halved
and seeded

2 garlic cloves

1 tbsp olive oil

1 tbsp lemon juice

1/2 cup fresh white bread
crumbs

salt and pepper

red bell pepper dip

Place the bell pepper halves and garlic in a pan and add just
enough water to cover. Bring to a boil, then lower the heat, cover,
and simmer gently for 10–15 minutes until softened and tender.
Drain and set aside to cool.

Coarsely chop the bell pepper halves and garlic and place in the
blender with the olive oil and lemon juice. Process to a smooth
purée.

Add the bread crumbs and process briefly until just combined.
Season to taste with salt and pepper. Transfer to a serving
bowl, cover with plastic wrap, and chill in the refrigerator until
required.

serves 6–8

9 oz/250 g whole beet

3¹/₂ oz/100 ml extra-virgin olive oil

4 oz/110 g roasted hazelnuts

2 garlic cloves, peeled

4 oz/110 g Parmesan cheese, freshly grated

salt and pepper

selection of crudités or bruschetta, to serve

beet & hazelnut pesto

Preheat the oven to 350°F/180°C.

Sprinkle the beet with a little salt and pepper, then drizzle with a small amount of the olive oil. Wrap the beet in foil and place in the oven. Cook for 1 hour. To test if the beet is cooked, pierce with a small knife; the blade should go in easily.

Remove the cooked beet from the oven and let cool. Peel away the skin and discard.

Place the hazelnuts and garlic in a food processor and process for 30 seconds.

Add the beet and salt and pepper to taste and process again, adding the remaining olive oil a little at a time, until completely combined.

Pour the pesto into a bowl and mix in the Parmesan cheese.

Serve with the crudités.